JUST *because*

POEMS

FRANCESCA THEODOROU

POEMS

FRANCESCA THEODOROU

MEMOIRS
Cirencester

Mereo Books

1A The Wool Market Dyer Street Cirencester Gloucestershire GL7 2PR
An imprint of Memoirs Publishing www.mereobooks.com

Just because: 978-1-909874-51-0

Copyright ©2014

Francesca Theodorou has asserted her right under the Copyright Designs and Patents
Act 1988 to be identified as the author of this work.

A CIP catalogue record for this book is available from the British Library.

This book is sold subject to the condition that it shall not by way of trade or otherwise
be lent, resold, hired out or otherwise circulated without the publisher's prior consent in
any form of binding or cover, other than that in which it is published and without a
similar condition, including this condition being imposed on the subsequent purchaser.

Cover design - Ray Lipscombe

The address for Memoirs Publishing Group Limited can be found at
www.memoirspublishing.com

The Memoirs Publishing Group Ltd Reg. No. 7834348

The Memoirs Publishing Group supports both The Forest Stewardship Council® (FSC®)
and the PEFC® leading international forest-certification organisations. Our books carrying
both the FSC label and the PEFC® and are printed on FSC®-certified paper. FSC® is the
only forest-certification scheme supported by the leading environmental organisations
including Greenpeace. Our paper procurement policy can be found at
www.memoirspublishing.com/environment

Typeset in 11/14pt Goudy
by Wiltshire Associates Publisher Services Ltd.
Printed and bound in Great Britain by Printondemand-Worldwide, Peterborough PE2 6XD

DEDICATION

I would like to dedicate my first book to my family and friends, who have always supported and encouraged me to write this book. They have always believed in me, even when I didn't. To Chris Newton and his team at Memoirs, who have helped to bring it to life with their expertise, knowledge and touch. To Phonso Camon. I have never met him because he lives in another country, but he always pushed and motivated me to write more every day and I called him my boss. And last but not least to my MuSeY, who was my inspiration. He may not have known it, but I'm sure he will now.

FOOL

Only a fool can fool another fool.

But at the end of it all, who are you actually fooling?

JUST BECAUSE

Just because I'm quiet it doesn't mean I don't have a lot to say.

Just because I appear happy it doesn't mean everything's OK.

Just because I forgive it doesn't mean I forget.

Just because I don't listen it doesn't mean I can't hear what you say.

And just because I don't show you my feelings it doesn't mean that I don't care.

CHANCES & CHOICES

I give everyone a chance.

Not because I'm trusting but because I don't believe everyone is born bad.

We've all felt pain which we can all understand.

I'll give you the rope, if you want to hang yourself with it you can.

Your choice will define you, not me.

YOU & ME

It's always been you...

It's just never been me...

So I found a better you with a new me...

REALISATION

You only realise just how much you like someone

When you realise just how much they like someone else.

MUSE

Whether you are good or bad for me it's always you.

Whether you are good or bad for me you are
my fucking muse!

WHO AM I?

I've become the person I said I'd never be again...

And the worst part of it all is that I never saw it coming.

ESCAPISM

You help me forget things... But who's going to help me forget you?

You are my escape... But I need an escape to escape you...

WISH

I wish my eyes could take pictures

Eat just by smelling food

And fall in love without breaking my heart.

AFRAID

I'm not afraid of flying, I'm afraid of falling.

I'm not afraid of living, I'm afraid of dying.

I'm not afraid of winning, I'm afraid of losing.

I'm not afraid of feeling, I'm afraid of hurting.

I'm not afraid of me, I'm afraid of you.

But one doesn't exist without the other.

You have to have the bad if you want the good.

I'm afraid that I'm not actually afraid at all.

CHAMELEON

Like a chameleon I adapt to my surroundings.

You're good to me I'll be good to you.

You're cold to me, sorry do I know you?

QUESTIONABLE

I question people…

Who do not question people…

CLOSED

There is nothing worse than a closed mind,

Closed mouth or a closed heart.

Even worse if you have all three.

TRUE COLOURS

People do not change.

Their true colours just start to shine through.

FLAWS

Choose your battles wisely.

You could be fighting a lost cause.

Be it with yourself or others, we all have our own flaws.

NOT ENOUGH

Too many caterpillars

Not enough butterflies.

MY GENERATION

Ladies & Gentlemen

A dying breed.

HEART & MIND

I like a clean heart with a dirty mind.

SOMETIMES

I can buy what I want but not what I need.
Sometimes I wish it was the other way round.

MEMORIES

Memories are all we are
And all that we will have left.

FRIENDS & LOVERS

I will never lose a friend for a lover.
But it's always good to gain a lover from a friend.

YOU SAY I SAY

You say I am a pessimist
I say I am a realist.
You say you are an optimist
I say you're delusional.

THE LITTLE THINGS

Appreciate all the little things in life

Like what people do for you to what you see in the world

A touch from your lover or a hug from your father

The smell of clean bed sheets or freshly baked bread

For one day you will look back and realise these were all the big things in life.

SECRET

I wanted to tell you all my secrets

But you became one of them.

GUILTY

We all are guilty of lying every day

It could be little white lies because you don't want to hurt somebody

Compulsive lies where you can't separate the real from the fake

But the biggest lies are the ones we tell ourselves for whatever reason

Until one day it smacks you in the face and you have to face yourself.

BROKEN & BREAKING

People who have been broken in the past want to
help fix broken people.

But sometimes they can break themselves trying to fix them.

And some broken people who are beyond repair
like to break other people

Because they don't know any better.

WANTING & NEEDING

There's a difference between wanting something
and needing something.

If you end up with what you want you will always
be needing for something more.

But if you end up with what you need you will
never be wanting for anything more.

I WANT I DON'T WANT

I don't want to be a nobody to just anybody.

I want to be a someone to somebody.

I want to be the reason they want to be better
and still not be bitter.

DO I?

Do I scare you because I can see right through you?

Through your show and tell that you try to impress with and hide behind that you seem to fool the fools with so easily.

Do I scare you because I can see right through it?

It doesn't impress me but yes I'm intrigued to see what other tricks you have up your sleeve.

Do I scare you because you don't actually scare me at all?

For I put on the exact same show, just with a different script.

DON'T FORGET ME

I know things and people change and your paths go on different ways.

Just please don't forget me.

I know there's nothing worse than being a nobody to your somebody.

Just please don't forget me.

And when that time comes for us to say our goodbyes and new hellos

Just please don't forget me.

WHAT WILL BE WILL BE

Whatever is meant to be will always find its way.

And if it doesn't find its way the way you hoped,
wanted or even wished for

It simply wasn't meant to be.

PRICE TO PAY

When you want something but don't need it

You sit and watch someone else love, take care of and feed it.

Sometimes you'll hate that you miss it so bad it's actually quite sad, when you want something so bad but don't actually need it.

There is a price to pay if you choose to stay, but right now it's getting too expensive.

So you need to ask yourself "how can I be expected to stay if I don't think I can actually afford it?"

SOMETIMES

When you badly crave something you start to see it in things that aren't actually there.

When you badly want something you'll turn a blind eye to what is actually there, just to feel that someone cares.

Sometimes feeling something is better than feeling nothing.

When you so badly want something any little sign will do, but I really wanted it to be you.

Of course you have to put in time and effort if you want it to work.

But you need to ask yourself first... Do you actually have anything to work with?

KNOTS & BUTTERFLIES

I get the butterflies in my stomach when I see you.

But then I get the knots in my stomach when you leave.

Come back one last time.

But I can't promise it won't make my heart bleed.

I AM

I am strong because I've been weak.

I am smart because I've been foolish.

I am closed because I've been open.

I am sceptical because I've been naive.

I don't trust easily because I have been tricked.

I am comfortable in my own skin because I've tried too much to impress the wrong people.

I found my way home because I've been lost too many times.

For every action there is a reaction.

We are all born the same but then made differently.

YOUR DAUGHTER

How can I be sitting right next to you and feel so far away?

How can I be sitting right next you and you can't even stroke my face?

All I want is for you to look at me... just me

The girl who has similar eyes to you, similar lips and even similar hair.

The girl who would love to hear you care.

If I was a boy would you love me more?

Or is showing love to a daughter a chore?

UN

If everybody wants it they can have it.

I won't stand in their way.

I'd rather have something Untouched, Unheard of and Unseen.

WHY? ...BECAUSE

Why did you leave?

Because you never asked me to stay.

Why didn't you tell me I was your number one?

Because you never made me feel that way.

Why don't you stay?

Because it's best I go.

Why are you so cold?

Because you turned me into stone.

Why won't you let me back in?

Because this isn't the Holiday Inn.

Please. Why won't you stay?

Because you pushed me too far away.

HEART, SOUL & MIND

Yes I am a giving person

It's in my heart, soul and mind.

Yes I will always give you a first chance and if you're lucky maybe a few more times.

It's in my heart, soul and mind

But don't you ever think that this makes me weak, dumb or blind.

For when I see a sign that you are not a giver and just a taker and a damn fool faker

You are the one who becomes weak, dumb and blind.

Because there is something missing in your heart, soul and mind.

WHERE ARE YOU?

Where are you?

I'm sitting here in this beautiful place waiting to see you.

The view is so peaceful and calm, how I should be in your arms.

How many more times must I be on my own without you?

THANK YOU

Thank you for never showing me any affection

It has taught me how beautiful a genuine hug should be.

Thank you for never praising or encouraging me

It has taught me to always push for that little bit more to feel great gratification inside of me.

Thank you for never telling me I was good, amazing or pretty

It has taught me to know that I am no better than anybody else I see.

And thank you for walking out on me

It has taught me to stand on my own two feet.

I DON'T WANT YOU

I don't want you too far away from me because I'll miss you.

I don't want you too close to me because you'll hurt me.

I don't want you to see too much of me because you might not like what's really underneath.

I don't want you to touch me because you'll awaken a secret part of me.

I don't want you to stay because it will kill me when you leave.

WHEN TO CRY

Yes I cry, I have no shame in saying it

For it's a great way to release.

But don't be mistaken and think that this makes weak.

But some people really aren't worth your tears, stress or energy.

ONCE UPON A TIME

When I was younger I used to think everything was so simple.

It was either right or wrong, day or night, black or white.

Then I grew a bit and realised some things that I thought were wrong felt so right, and the things that felt right became so wrong.

And the things that would scare me in the night when I was a child were nowhere near as scary as the things
I saw in the daylight with my eyes wide open without my blanket to hide under.

And last but not least that nothing is black and white.

There is that grey area that people forget to see, which is cloudy and misty.

The place where it's hard to recognise and understand each other, let alone see.

HEART, BRAIN, BODY, MIND & SOUL

When it comes to matters of your heart you play a very weird and closed part.

When it comes to matters of your brain you seem so well contained.

When it comes to matters of your body you're giving it everybody.

When it comes to matters of your mind this you need to find.

When it comes to matters of your soul you try too much to control and you are left with just a hole.

SHE IS NOT ME

If you want someone just to agree with you to please you

Then she is not me.

If you want someone to satisfy you physically and to shut her mouth

Then I am afraid she is not me.

If you want someone to walk behind you and never redirect you when you can't see clearly

Then she is definitely not me.

I am who I am

And who I am is me.

TORN

When you are torn between two, who do you choose?

The one you can be yourself with but who is no
good for you?

Or the one who is good for you but who can't
actually see you?

The one who makes you feel at ease but who is
so hard to please?

Or the one who has their head screwed on but yet whose
heart is still switched off?

The one who is full of surprises and always arises?

Or the one who is full of potential but has no credentials?

They say when you're torn between two to opt for the latter

But it's not that easy when it comes to the heart's matter.

BITCH OR BLESSING

Time can be a bitch or she can be a blessing.

She can make you suffer slowly but she will give you a lesson.

You'll only appreciate her when she has left you

And you will look back and be thankful.

The only problem is, you won't know which it is until she
has passed you.

SOMETIMES IT'S EASIER

When he tells her he loves her, she'll always question why

Sometimes it's easier to believe you're not loveable than to conceive you are and yet still nobody loves you anyway.

When he tells her she's beautiful she'll always say,
are you blind?

Sometimes it's easier to believe you're not when
nobody has ever made her feel that way.

When he tells her I'm always here for you, just
stop pushing me away!

She'll say to him it's easier to do the pushing then
to watch you walk away.

When he's finally reached his limit and turns to say goodbye

She won't say a word to him or even put up a fight.

Sadly she's been accustomed to this and will just
watch him disappear into the night.

FACES

It's so hard to take people for face value nowadays

Especially when they have so many.

OWN YOUR SKIN

Fake hair and fake tits

Fake eyelashes and fake lips

Bit of Botox here

Bit of suction there

Where else on your natural body is there left to make disappear?

Why do you have to put these foreign bodies into your body?

There's a difference between enhancing your beauty and totally killing it.

Until you are comfortable in your own skin

No matter how much work you have done to it

It will never be enough

And you will never be satisfied on the outside

Until you accept who you are from the inside.

KNOCK KNOCK

I'm always looking out for someone new

Because if I don't I always end up running back to you.

I'm always looking for that little spark

To make up for your charming mark.

But why is it when I have finally forgotten you

I hear a knock on my door of a reminder of you pleading for once more?

ONE

One look when you lock eyes

One touch that gives you butterflies

One smile to make you weak

One deep conversation when you speak

One kind gesture that makes you tender

One kiss that makes you surrender

One amazing hug like you've never felt

One little giggle that when you hear makes you melt

One hello for all the above to start

One goodbye to end it all and depart

BUT

I like it

But I don't love it.

I want it

But I don't need it.

I'll be fine

But I'm not.

It hasn't even started

But it's done.

It doesn't matter

But it does.

SECRET TREASURE

I can still feel your touch, your firm grip on my hips.

I can still taste your tongue, skin and lips.

I can still hear your sound, like my favourite song on repeat.

I can still see your fierce deep gaze every time I go to sleep.

It's a bitter-sweet memory filled with pain and pleasure

But it will always be my secret treasure.

YOU REALLY DID

I tried to save you I really did
Day by day, bit by bit.
Instead you ended up killing me
Day by day, bit by bit.
I tried to put you back together, I really did
Piece by piece, slowly and gently.
Instead you tore me apart
Piece by piece, slowly and gently.
I tried to fix you, I really did
With every touch and every kiss.
Instead you broke me
With every touch and every kiss.
You really did.

PRECIOUS

You are more precious to me than any gem, stone or gold

For your protection I would sell my soul.

I could watch you sleep for days on end dreaming away so peacefully,

I could stroke your face and look into your innocent eyes which shine so brightly.

I could hold your hand forever to guide you while you grow,

And love you forever because you are my heart and soul.

IF YOU WANT TO

If you want to know how I feel about you

Listen to what I can't, don't and won't say.

If you want to know how much I care for you

Feel it when I'm close to you, touch and stroke you.

If you want to hear the words I long to say to you

Listen to the music I play day after day.

SECRET SHELTER

In a world that is forever changing it's hard to recognise anybody I know.

They all look the same and are so boring and lame.

I might be expecting too much, but why is it so hard to meet someone with a common touch?

So I'll go and hide in my secret shelter

Until this world full of fools is filled with something better.

THE MOTH & THE FLAME

She was his light to his dark

Even though his world was very bad.

He was her dream in her reality

Even though she was very sad.

He was the moth and she was the flame

And in their special moments they were free but tamed.

I HAVE BEEN THERE BEFORE

He wasn't my first love

And I don't think he'll be my last

For his heart is broken and damaged and wrapped in a cast.

I tell him the only way to fix it:

"You have to use it."

Instead he just looks at me, frowns

And says "are you having a laugh?"

The longer I am around him

The harder it is to breathe

For he uses mine as a splint

As I wear my heart on my sleeve.

As I turn to walk away and say goodbye he asks me

"How can I be so sure?"

I turn and say to him

"Because I have been there before".

USING

The energy between them was so electric
But at the end it became too toxic.
One touch from him could send her soul on fire
One touch from her was all he wanted and desired.
She made him feel at peace
He made her feel at ease.
They pushed and pulled from each other
Always trying to feel higher
Using one another
To fulfil their desires.
One drained the other, causing pain to each other
They broke and crushed it until there was nothing left
With feelings that were unexpressed.

IGNORANCE IS BLISS

When you can find peace in the madness
Patience in the sadness
And dismiss Judas's kiss
That's when ignorance is bliss.

LONELINESS

Loneliness can make you do the craziest things.

Stay when you should go,

Put up and shut up when you should stand up and speak up.

Loneliness will have you confusing love for being used and abused.

Loneliness can make you do the craziest things.

Make you keep running to somebody who doesn't truly have your back,

Keep giving yourself emotionally and physically without them giving anything back.

Loneliness will have you confusing love for lust, or just a simple fuck.

SECRET GARDEN

If you want me, then claim me

Before someone else tames me

I am not playing your game

For when they do you will still want me.

And when you are in your secret garden

You will hold your head down in shame

For you will only have yourself to blame

When I have finally walked away.

THE EYES

I used to think what made eyes beautiful was their colour.

Sparkling green to piercing blue

From hazy hazel with a light caramel tinged with emeralds,

Or the deepest darkest brown you could drown in.

But it's not.

It's the eyes that when you look into you
immediately lock with,

The eyes that tell a secret that only you can read,

The eyes that you connect with consistently,

The eyes that give you that feeling of
familiarity and sincerity,

The eyes that are wild but filled with the laughter of a child,

They're the eyes that I love to see.

DEAD IN THE MORNING

Why are you telling me now that I'm dying?

"Because I couldn't allow myself to believe you'd love me,
I thought you were lying.

Please don't hate me, I wish I didn't wait."

But there's nothing I can do for you now

How?

I'll be dead in the morning.

BRING YOU TO LIFE

If I write about you, will that bring you to life?

If I write about you, will you end my strife?

With every letter, will you make things better?

If I list what I long for, will that make you exist?

With every word out spoken, will you fix all that is broken?

I don't want a borrowed hero who can't be here for tomorrow

Just please send me someone to end all my sorrow.

SILLY ME

She might be able to give your eyes a treat

But can she make your heart skip a beat?

She might be able to feed you whatever you want

But can she feed you what you need?

I know what your answers will be

Silly me, to expect any depth from someone so shallow.

ALLY

Physically full

Emotionally starved

Mentally drained

Spiritually lost.

MAKE BELIEVE

Sometimes it's easier to fake a smile

And pretend everything's OK for a while.

Sometimes it's easier to say "oh it's nothing"

Than to say "oh it's everything"

For in that moment of the make-believe,

The fake and the lies

You might just feel it.

PAINKILLER

A drug or medicine for relieving pain

To make you numb and release the physical and mental chains.

Primarily it's temporary

And you are mine.

NEW GENERATION

In this new generation, with so many temptations,
situations and separations

People are scared to lay down any solid and
genuine foundations.

They will hurt you first for their own sanity and protection.

Just as in sports the best form of defence is attack

But this isn't a game

Which is why this generation is a shame,
a disgrace and whack!

UNPHYSICAL HEALER

A writer isn't one person

A writer is many people rolled into one.

A writer doesn't write because they are forced to

A writer writes because they have, need and love to.

A writer writes to express the unspoken words, thoughts
and emotions of the reader

To be the unphysical healer.

If they can touch at least one person, then their job is done.

THE REST OF ME

It wasn't when you spat in my face and made me
feel like I was a disgrace

It wasn't when you tore my clothes off and called me a whore

It wasn't when you beat me black and blue
I knew we were through

It wasn't when you tried to take my life from me,
like I was no value to you

It was when I saw the thrill in your eyes from the fear in
mine of everything you had done to me

And if I had stayed one more day you would've
got the best of me

I could take all the physical stuff you gave me

But there was no way I was giving you the rest of me

Even though I crawled out of there on my hands and knees

With tears and blood running down my cheeks

There was no fucking way you were taking the rest of me!

FORGIVE ME

I really hope and pray you believe me when I say

"I did what I had to do because I thought it was best for you"

I really hope and pray you believe me when I say

"It hurt me more than it hurt you"

I wasn't ready for you or for what tore my soul

I never once imagined this is how my first child would've been conceived into this world.

I wanted you to be born in happiness, love and bliss

Not a place full of sadness, anger and mistrust.

I really hope and pray you believe me when I say

"Wherever you may be... please, if you can... forgive me."

www.ingramcontent.com/pod-product-compliance
Lightning Source LLC
Chambersburg PA
CBHW061347040426
42444CB00011B/3125